READING CORNER

Camping Trip

Written by
**Deborah
Chancellor**

Photographed by
**Chris
Fairclough**

W
FRANKLIN WATTS
LONDON•SYDNEY

Deborah Chancellor

"When I was little, I used to make camps in the woods with my sisters. Now, I go camping with my children!"

Chris Fairclough

"I've been taking photos for books for almost 30 years and have visited 53 countries. Every day is different!"

Camping Trip

A non-fiction
recount text

First published in 2004 by
Franklin Watts
96 Leonard Street
London
EC2A 4XD

Franklin Watts Australia
45–51 Huntley Street
Alexandria
NSW 2015

Text © Deborah Chancellor 2004
Photographs © Franklin Watts 2004

A CIP catalogue record for this book is available
from the British Library.

ISBN 0 7496 5310 8 (hbk)
ISBN 0 7496 5374 4 (pbk)

Series Editor: Jackie Hamley
Series Advisors: Dr Barrie Wade, Dr Hilary Minns
Design: Peter Scoulding
Photographs: Chris Fairclough

The author and publisher would especially like to thank
Sharon and Yasmin Bowen, Kaya Allen and Rosie and
Nick Gordon for giving their help and time so generously.

Printed in Hong Kong / China

I packed my bag to
go camping.

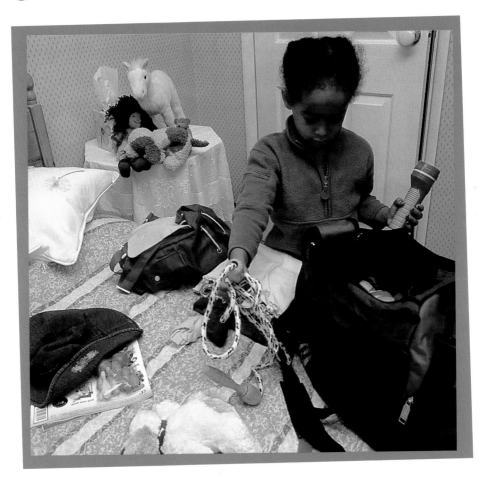

I took some
food and
drink.

My friend
Kaya came
with me.

Mum helped us find a dry, flat spot.

We pushed
the poles into
the tent.

13

We lifted the tent up.

Then we put in the pegs.

We threw the cover over the top.

We pegged the cover down.

We pulled the ropes tight.

Then Mum
fell asleep
in the tent...

So we went
to camp in
my bedroom!

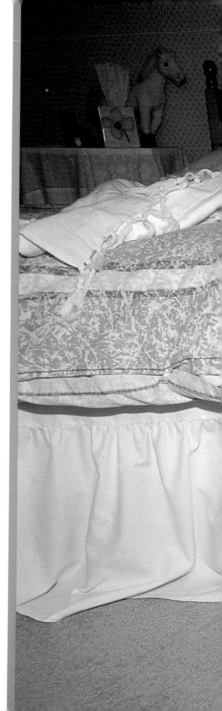

Notes for parents and teachers

READING CORNER has been structured to provide maximum support for new readers. The stories may be used by adults for sharing with young children. Primarily, however, the stories are designed for newly independent readers, whether they are reading these books in bed at night, or in the reading corner at school or in the library.

Starting to read alone can be a daunting prospect. READING CORNER helps by providing visual support and repeating words and phrases, while making reading enjoyable. These books will develop confidence in the new reader, and encourage a love of reading that will last a lifetime!

If you are reading this book with a child, here are a few tips:

1. Make reading fun! Choose a time to read when you and the child are relaxed and have time to share the story.

2. Encourage children to reread the story, and to retell the story in their own words, using the illustrations to remind them what has happened.

3. Give praise! Remember that small mistakes need not always be corrected.

READING CORNER covers three grades of early reading ability, with three levels at each grade. Each level has a certain number of words per story, indicated by the number of bars on the spine of the book, to allow you to choose the right book for a young reader:

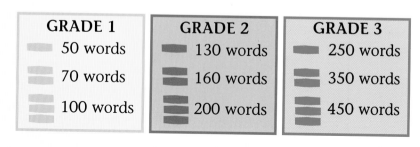

GRADE 1	GRADE 2	GRADE 3
50 words	130 words	250 words
70 words	160 words	350 words
100 words	200 words	450 words